THE HUMAN BEHIND THE HERO

CHRIS PRATT
IS STAR-LORD®

BY KATIE KAWA

Gareth Stevens
PUBLISHING

Please visit our website, www.garethstevens.com. For a free color catalog of all our high-quality books, call toll free 1-800-542-2595 or fax 1-877-542-2596.

Cataloging-in-Publication Data

Names: Kawa, Katie, author.
Title: Chris Pratt is Star-Lord / Katie Kawa.
Description: New York : Gareth Stevens Publishing, [2020] | Series: The human behind the hero | Includes index.
Identifiers: LCCN 2019014325| ISBN 9781538248270 (pbk.) | ISBN 9781538248294 (library bound) | ISBN 9781538248287 (6 pack)
Subjects: LCSH: Pratt, Chris, 1979–Juvenile literature. | Motion picture actors and actresses–United States–Biography–Juvenile literature. | Television actors and actresses–United States–Biography–Juvenile literature.
Classification: LCC PN2287.P66 K39 2020 | DDC 791.4302/8092 [B] –dc23
LC record available at https://lccn.loc.gov/2019014325

First Edition

Published in 2020 by
Gareth Stevens Publishing
111 East 14th Street, Suite 349
New York, NY 10003

Designer: Sarah Liddell
Editor: Katie Kawa

Photo credits: Cover, p. 1 Tinseltown/Shutterstock.com; halftone texture used throughout gn8/Shutterstock.com; comic frame used throughout KID_A/Shutterstock.com; p. 5 Alberto E. Rodriguez/Getty Images Entertainment/GettyImages; p. 7 Suzi Pratt/Contributor/WireImage/GettyImages; p. 9 Featureflash Photo Agency/Shutterstock.com; p. 11 Albert L. Ortega/Contirbutor/WireImage/Getty Images; p. 13 Jesse Grant/Contributor/WireImage/Getty Images; p. 15 Frazer Harrison/Staff/Getty Images Entertainment/Getty Images; p. 17 Andrew Toth/Stringer/Getty Images Entertainment/Getty Images; p. 19 Ian West - PA Images/Contributor/PA Images/Getty Images; p. 21 Samir Hussein/Contributor/WireImage/Getty Images; p. 23 Jon Kopaloff/Stringer/FilmMagic/Getty Images; p. 25 Todd Williamson/Contributor/Getty Images Entertainment/Getty Images; p. 27 Kevin Winter/Staff/Getty Images Entertainment/Getty Images; p. 29 Kevork Djansezian/Stringer/Getty Images Entertainment/Getty Images.

Printed in the United States of America

Some of the images in this book illustrate individuals who are models. The depictions do not imply actual situations or events.

CPSIA compliance information: Batch #CW20GS: For further information contact Gareth Stevens, New York, New York at 1-800-542-2595.

CONTENTS

AN UNLIKELY HERO

The Guardians of the Galaxy
are a group of unlikely heroes
who've become big hits in
Marvel movies. The star of those
movies—Chris Pratt—is an unlikely
hero too. His **journey** from an
unknown actor to the superhero
Star-Lord shows that hard work
pays off!

GUARDIANS OF THE GALAXY

WORLD PREMIERE

BEHIND THE SCENES

STAR-LORD IS ALSO KNOWN BY THE NAME PETER QUILL. HE FIRST APPEARED IN MARVEL COMIC BOOKS IN 1976, WHICH WAS 3 YEARS BEFORE CHRIS PRATT WAS BORN.

CHRIS AS A KID

Chris Pratt was born on June 21, 1979. His full name is Christopher, but most people call him Chris. When Chris was in high school, he told people he was going to be famous, but he didn't know then how it was going to happen.

BEHIND THE SCENES
CHRIS WAS BORN IN MINNESOTA,
BUT HIS FAMILY MOVED TO
WASHINGTON STATE WHEN HE WAS YOUNG.
HE BECAME A BIG FAN OF THE SEATTLE
SEAHAWKS FOOTBALL TEAM BECAUSE
THEY PLAY IN WASHINGTON.

FROM WAITER TO ACTOR

Chris spent time working as a waiter in Hawaii before he became a star. One day at work, he met an actress and director named Rae Dawn Chong. She liked him and decided to put him in her **short film** *Cursed Part 3.*

BEHIND THE SCENES

ALTHOUGH CHRIS MAKES A LOT OF MONEY NOW, HE WAS HOMELESS FOR A TIME WHILE HE WAS LIVING IN HAWAII. CHRIS DIDN'T MAKE A LOT OF MONEY THERE, SO HE LIVED IN A VAN.

TV TIME

When Chris first started acting, he got a lot of work on TV shows that teens watched. In 2002, he started acting on the TV show *Everwood*. When *Everwood* ended in 2006, Chris joined the cast of a show called *The O.C.*

BEHIND THE SCENES

CHRIS HAS ALSO ACTED IN MANY MOVIES. SOME OF HIS MOST WELL-KNOWN PARTS IN MOVIES BEFORE *GUARDIANS OF THE GALAXY* WERE IN THE 2011 MOVIE *MONEYBALL* AND THE 2012 MOVIE *ZERO DARK THIRTY*.

A FUNNY GUY

Chris started working on the TV show *Parks and Recreation* in 2009. He played a funny character named Andy Dwyer until the show ended in 2015. This was good practice for the funny moments in *Guardians of the Galaxy*.

BEHIND THE SCENES

ON *PARKS AND RECREATION*, CHRIS'S CHARACTER, ANDY, WAS IN A BAND AND WAS OFTEN SHOWN SINGING SONGS. CHRIS LOVES MUSIC AND IS VERY GOOD AT PLAYING *GUITAR*.

THE BEST CHOICE

When Chris was working on *Parks and Recreation*, he heard about *Guardians of the Galaxy*. He wanted to play Star-Lord, but he had to try out for the part first. James Gunn, who directed the movie, knew right away Chris was the best choice!

JAMES GUNN

BEHIND THE SCENES

THE GUARDIANS OF THE GALAXY IN MARVEL MOVIES ARE STAR-LORD, GROOT, GAMORA, DRAX THE DESTROYER, ROCKET RACCOON, AND MANTIS. THEY'RE ALSO SOMETIMES HELPED BY GAMORA'S ADOPTED SISTER, NEBULA.

15

GETTING IN SHAPE

Playing a superhero isn't easy. Chris had to work hard to get ready to play Star-Lord. He ate healthier and worked with a trainer for months to get strong and fit. He swam, ran, and did other kinds of exercise to get in shape.

BEHIND THE SCENES

CHRIS FINISHED A KIND OF RACE CALLED AN IRONMAN 70.3 IN 2015. IN THIS RACE, HE HAD TO RUN, SWIM, AND RIDE A BIKE FOR A TOTAL OF 70.3 MILES (113.1 KM). HE DID THIS TO RAISE MONEY FOR VETERANS.

17

SUCCESS AS STAR-LORD

On August 1, 2014, fans were able to watch *Guardians of the Galaxy* for the first time. Many people weren't sure what to expect, but it became one of the year's most successful movies. In fact, it made more than $700 million around the world!

MARVEL
GUARDIANS
OF THE GALAXY

BEHIND THE SCENES

CHRIS HAS ALSO BEEN PART OF
THE *LEGO* MOVIES. HE WAS
THE VOICE OF EMMET BRICKOWSKI IN
2014'S *THE LEGO MOVIE* AND 2019'S
THE LEGO MOVIE 2: THE SECOND PART.

VOL. 2

Chris and the rest of the cast soon went back to work making another *Guardians of the Galaxy* movie. *Guardians of the Galaxy Vol. 2* came out on May 5, 2017. It was even more successful than the first movie, making more than $800 million around the world.

MARVEL STUDIOS

ZOE SALDANA

BEHIND THE SCENES

THE OTHER ACTORS IN THE GUARDIANS OF THE GALAXY MOVIES ARE FAMOUS TOO. FOR EXAMPLE, ZOE SALDANA, WHO PLAYS GAMORA, HAS BEEN IN THE *STAR TREK* MOVIES AND THE MOVIE *AVATAR*.

TEAMING UP

Star-Lord and the other

Guardians of the Galaxy

teamed up with the Avengers in

the 2018 movie *Avengers: Infinity*

War. The next year, Chris played

Star-Lord again in the movie

Avengers: Endgame. These

were two of the most successful

superhero movies of all time!

BEHIND THE SCENES

AVENGERS: INFINITY WAR AND AVENGERS: ENDGAME STARRED THREE ACTORS NAMED CHRIS! CHRIS PRATT JOINED CHRIS HEMSWORTH, WHO PLAYED THOR, AND CHRIS EVANS, WHO PLAYED CAPTAIN AMERICA, IN THESE MOVIES.

23

WHAT'S NEXT?

Chris worked with Tom Holland, who plays Spider-Man, on the *Avengers* movies. He also worked with him on the **animated** movie *Onward*, which uses both of their voices. After *Onward*, Chris plans to star in the third *Guardians of the Galaxy* movie.

TOM HOLLAND

BEHIND THE SCENES

CHRIS ALSO WORKS WITH DINOSAURS! HE PLAYED OWEN GRADY IN THE 2015 MOVIE *JURASSIC WORLD* AND THE 2018 MOVIE *JURASSIC WORLD: FALLEN KINGDOM*. HE'S ALSO WORKING ON A THIRD *JURASSIC WORLD* MOVIE.

25

HELPING KIDS

When Chris isn't traveling into outer space as Star-Lord, he's often traveling to different **hospitals** to spend time with kids who are sick. Helping kids is important to Chris because he's a dad. His son Jack was born in August 2012.

Kids Wish Network

I MADE DAGEN'S WISH COME TRUE

BEHIND THE SCENES

WHEN CHRIS VISITS KIDS IN THE HOSPITAL, HE SOMETIMES DRESSES UP AS STAR-LORD. HE KEPT HIS STAR-LORD JACKET SO HE COULD WEAR IT ON THESE SPECIAL VISITS.

BEYOND THE BIG SCREEN

Chris Pratt loves playing the superhero Star-Lord, but he also knows there's more to life than making movies. His family means a lot to him, and so does helping others. He knows that's what makes someone a real hero!

BEHIND THE SCENES

CHRIS ENJOYS SPENDING TIME OUTSIDE DOING THINGS SUCH AS FISHING. HE ALSO HAS A FARM IN WASHINGTON WHERE HE GROWS FRUITS AND VEGETABLES. HE RAISES ANIMALS SUCH AS SHEEP TOO.

TIMELINE

1979 CHRIS PRATT IS BORN ON JUNE 21.

2002 CHRIS GETS HIS FIRST BIG ACTING JOB ON THE TV SHOW *EVERWOOD*.

2009 CHRIS BEGINS PLAYING ANDY DWYER ON *PARKS AND RECREATION*.

2012 CHRIS'S SON JACK IS BORN.

2014 CHRIS IS PART OF *THE LEGO MOVIE* AND PLAYS STAR-LORD FOR THE FIRST TIME IN *GUARDIANS OF THE GALAXY*.

2015 CHRIS STARS IN *JURASSIC WORLD*.

2017 *GUARDIANS OF THE GALAXY VOL. 2* COMES OUT IN MAY.

2018 CHRIS PLAYS STAR-LORD AGAIN IN *AVENGERS: INFINITY WAR* AND PLAYS OWEN GRADY AGAIN IN *JURASSIC WORLD: FALLEN KINGDOM*.

2019 *THE LEGO MOVIE 2: THE SECOND PART* AND *AVENGERS: ENDGAME* OPEN.

FOR MORE INFORMATION

BOOKS

Abdo, Kenny. *Chris Pratt*. Minneapolis, MN: Abdo Zoom, 2019.

Bray, Adam. *Marvel Studios 101: All Your Questions Answered*. New York, NY: DK Publishing, 2018.

Jones, Nick. *Marvel Guardians of the Galaxy: The Ultimate Guide to the Cosmic Outlaws*. New York, NY: DK Publishing, 2017.

WEBSITES

IMDb: Chris Pratt
www.imdb.com/name/nm0695435/
The Internet Movie Database has a list of all of Chris Pratt's movies, as well as facts about his life.

Marvel: Star-Lord
www.marvel.com/characters/star-lord-peter-quill
The official Marvel website offers fun facts about Star-Lord in both the movies and comics.

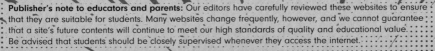

GLOSSARY

adopted: made part of a family

animated: made up of drawings or computer images that appear to move

guitar: a musical instrument that generally has six strings and is played by plucking or strumming

hospital: a place where people are cared for when they are very sick or hurt

jacket: a light and short coat

journey: an act of traveling from one place to another or moving from one part of life to another

short film: a movie that is commonly less than 40 minutes long

veteran: someone who fought in a war

INDEX